A Dream Come True

by

Daniel G. Montejano

Bloomington, IN      Milton Keynes, UK

authorHOUSE®

AuthorHouse™
1663 Liberty Drive, Suite 200
Bloomington, IN 47403
www.authorhouse.com
Phone: 1-800-839-8640

AuthorHouse™ UK Ltd.
500 Avebury Boulevard
Central Milton Keynes, MK9 2BE
www.authorhouse.co.uk
Phone: 08001974150

First published by AuthorHouse   5/1/2007

ISBN: 978-1-4343-1083-5 (sc)

Printed in the United States of America
Bloomington, Indiana

This book is printed on acid-free paper.

Heart

When it comes to love,
we tend to let our heart
believe that words are stronger
than our heart,
so it's easy to see
how people are torn apart.

One Day

I knew one day…
You'd close your eyes,
and make me the tears in your eyes.
All the tears I cry,
are the questions of why?
Thought I'd have you know,
as I leave,
I'll catch my tears,
and refuse to ever let you go.
I'll always be in a place,
you forgot you have inside of you.
The tears you've cried,
were all the lies you ever made me believe inside.

In Heaven

In heaven, there are no dreams and broken hearts.
Resting in each others arms,
we'll belong to each other's hearts.
I wish I could turn back,
and erase all the things we did,
and ever said;
I can't define how sweet and kind
I found you to be in my mind.
I can describe all the pain that still remains;
It's easy to say none begins to ease,
so I look up towards the heavens
and see your precious face,
and all the memories that will never leave;
I'll see you again when we meet in heaven,
where there are no dreams and broken hearts.
Resting in each other's arms,
we'll belong to each other's hearts.

Fairytale

I often think of you at night
and wonder if you'll ever be mine again?
Through my eyes, a fairytale lies.
You're beautiful and kind, precious and sweet.
It's as you only exist within my dreams
and every time I see your face,
I feel that special place inside my heart.
I know you're the best girl any guy could ever have!
Through my eyes,
I told you a fairytale lies.

Must Be In Love

No amount of fire or flames
can ruin our days;
Our hearts continue to beat
and never skip a beat;
We must be in love,
it exceeds beyond the sea,
and when we suffer pain and loss,
even then we know...
We must be in love.

Once More

I never thought my life could be clean until
you showed me better dreams.
Rather it be in the middle of the day or late at night,
you lit my life,
and held both my hands;
Then with a gentle look,
you took my heart.
From that moment on,
I knew I loved you with all my heart.
I would give up my world,
just to hold you once more.

More Than a Passing Friend

I miss your soft lips,
and the way I could feel you smiling when we kiss.
We still talk every now and then,
but we aren't even half as close as we used to be.
I'm sorry for the things I did,
but I can't take it back.
Knowing our love is now behind a closed door;
How can I tell you what I feel for you?
You won't believe it! Better I stay mute,
and yet I still wish to tell you of my love,
as something more than just a passing friend…

God's Gift to Me

You've taken my life away from me!
It killed me deep!
I will now become someone I should never be!
I thought we were meant to be?
Our hearts were forever kept,
you will always be my first true love.
I guess you want to move on,
but please hold on before you move on.
Remember, you are kept in my heart!
I got torn apart or did I just fall apart?
I so deserve to die only God won't take my life.
I have nothing more in this life.
Why can't I go to the other side?
My heart has been torn from inside of me.
You were God's gift to me.
You were everything inside of me.
I hope you will always keep that special ring
until we reach the end.
I hate to say the final bye,
You were God's gift to me.
Even before I saw you in this world,
remember you were God's gift to me.
I love you!!
Now and forever!!

A Dream Comes True

Every day when I see a special someone,
I know all my dreams have come true.
To the very purist,
You make it seem nothings impossible.
You're a dream come true!
It's your love that made my dreams come true.
Never will I ever have to close my eyes
to have another dream,
please believe that I only keep you in my heart,
nothing can take us apart,
so death will never do us part.
I'm always there day or night, rain or shine.
Anything you say I'll do!
You're an angel of God!
So sweet and hot!
I've been blessed by and angel of God;
He knew I would love you best.
He chose you to make my dreams come true.

The Love for You

Rest your head and close your eyes,
as all I do is think of you,
although I look for you in every doorway,
I can only hear the wind blow.
Is this telling me to put my thoughts to sleep?
Well, the time came and went so fast,
a stranger you were once,
the love for you is my reason to be,
or when I'm feeling pain,
the love for you makes it rain;
So all the pain is driven away.
I'll find you one day standing in a doorway.

My Love

I take your hand to see my life flash before my eyes.
You take me to a place so high beyond the sky,
nice and bright, we keep each other's hearts nice and tight.
With each other's love for one another,
I believe nothing more except our true love.
You make me feel like a million dollar man!
You only give me the very best!
I'm glad to say it's not a dream or even make belief,
even though you like to flirt,
we keep each other's hearts nice and tight.
I try not to start a fight,
I try to make our hearts twice as bright.
Always say your mine,
like the time we were out on the street that night,
and you were by me for the first time in my life.
I wish I could have told you it was love at first sight;
You've changed my life before everyone's eyes.
I hope you'll always be mine,
even when I graduate from Iraan high…

Personal Dream

I think of you a lot,
so many thoughts, you rest in them all.
I just don't know who you are!
Yet, I have a nearness to you,
but, not one memory of you,
and I still have precious thoughts of you.
Though I've never seen you before in my life,
or ever heard a single story of you…
Could this be a false belief?
No such thing as a personal dream,
let me forget the things that were,
and the things that weren't meant to be;
I still do not know to this day
what to say except,
I just don't know who you are?
How the only question is…
Whether I shall see you again?
But, what more good would it do?
I'm just in a personal dream.

It's Not A Dream

I close my eyes, I find you in my mind,
I try to sleep and there you are in my dreams.
All the memories won't ever set us free,
we've just begun the start of something new,
something very few can do.
I know you haven't let me go,
don't forget we keep something special.
Please always believe and neither one of us will ever leave.
I believe you do see me in your dreams,
that's the only place you can keep me.
When you sleep we shall always meet.
I hate to see you sad and when your not there for me,
it's hard not to cry.
I'm left alone in the black wishing...
I still had you to come back to.
I'll stand tall, won't ever fall,
I'll always be waiting for your call;
So then I can ask you to be by my side,
and you hold my hand through our journey in life.
One day, I'll find myself on my knee,
before your very eyes to try and find the courage
to ask you to be my wife...

Looking At You

I realize as I look at you,
I really don't have a clue,
on how to make it right;
All the nice things we said are in the past,
I thought our relationship would never end,
but that was all fake and pretend,
and then one day it was all so blue.
It's breaking my heart to walk away from you,
even though I'm not your boyfriend, I'll still be there,
that's not going to change even though we're apart.
Maybe we will be together again if it was meant to be.

Everything's Gone

I thought I was strong,
till the day it all went wrong.
You told me,
the love for me was suddenly lost
and the gleam of light,
in our eyes were broke apart,
all the sparks evaporated from our hearts.
Everything we built
was torn apart,
as our hearts were driven away,
our tears dried away.
I thought I was strong,
till the day it all went wrong.
You left me all alone,
trying to figure out
why you smashed my heart?
Now I ask God, to
help keep me strong.

Thinking of You

I was thinking of you last night
and all the times we shared.
My feelings for you will never change
and if you ever wonder why...
I don't know what I'll say?
Things go wrong no matter what I do;
We met a long time ago in school;
I remember our first kiss and think about our last.
You took another man after stealing my heart!
It broke in two...
One to be stepped into the Earth,
the other for you;
Now I just want to know...
How much longer my heart will be hallow?

Toots

Thinking about my Toots?
How you used to be my world,
the way you inspired my life,
to this day I still cry.
Because of you, I'll never see a penitentiary,
wish you were still here,
to help me wipe away the tears I've cried.
But, I thank you for helping me
make a better life.
I hold you dearly deep inside my heart,
as I have from the start.
I'll love you forever,
with all my heart!
I'll always see your face
sparkle with the stars.

A Whisper

Of all the girls' I've ever met,
you're the one I can't forget.
You were always there for everything
and every time I heard you speak,
it was like humming birds sing.
How much I love you….
You'll never really know.
I've learned the full meaning of love
and I'll whisper your name,
when no one is near,
so low that only you can hear.
Regardless, our feelings are always
true and real.

The Unforgettable

Why can't I forget about you and heal?
We gave each other a few last kisses,
now you act like I was never of existence to you.
It's been misery…
Even when we were together, misery was there;
I try to forget our past,
something in my heart says other wise.
No questions asked…
In heaven we won't be denied,
we'll hold each other's hands,
and walk the sky.
I guess that's why,
I wake remembering our past.

Missing You

You have a dream, could it ever be real?
The things you feel and see, ever be?
The night you kissed my lips,
and whipped all my tears,
you held my hand and whispered…
You belong to my heart.
Now we find ourselves ever far,
I miss looking in your eyes,
and before I call it a night,
I tell you goodnight.
I wish I could kiss you before I hit the lights,
when I wake, I'm still empty inside.
I just pray you haven't forgotten me in your heart;
It's true! Your face is carved by the angels.
Separated for now,
only faith shall have it.

Lust

We gave each other so much trust,
thought we were in love,
it was only to be lust.
All the fun we thought we had,
all the times we told each other we cared,
till the last time we held each other.
Until the last time…
we decided to kiss one another,
not once could we ever call it love,
our hearts tricked us into lust.

Remembering

I remember all the worries we spent together,
and all the memories we hold with each other;
I can even close my eyes,
and go back to the first time I took your hand;
I stared you in the eyes,
thinking my life was complete,
but instead, how I cry myself to sleep,
and remember you through my dreams…
Then I wake up screaming,
because when I'm dreaming,
I hear you whispering…
I have trouble remembering who you are?

Believing

Believing there was something in your smile,
that drove me wild and fell in love;
It was God giving me another life,
to turn around and make right,
to take your hand and start a new life,
even after we separate,
I'll stand alone in the rain
and let it pour down my face.
I think it's too late because I'm left alone in the rain
but if I can show that I can stand alone,
then together we'll go to the heavens.

Misunderstanding

Here's the thing...
You told me you'd be mine forever,
dedicated me all those love songs,
made me believe that I was all you ever wanted,
and kept me going;
I had a misunderstanding?
Filled my head with so many stories,
and left me standing with my hand over my heart.
It would be the last time
we'd ever meet
and the last lie you'd
ever make me believe.

Living in Silence

Holding me so soft,
without you I'd be lost.
Falling in love with you
came at a great personal cost;
You showed me the stars
and told me one day
you'd even say, "I do."
Now we act like we never dated a single day,
or ever speak of the things we used to say,
as if everything's ok.
It won't be long,
till you remember my face.
We'll wait for one another at the gates.

Here's What I Know

Here's what I know…
You're beautiful and sweet,
it was as if I were in a dream.
You know I could sit and say you're so FINE,
but through my eyes I
saw someone that swept me off my feet.
I bet you disagree,
but this is what I know…
Didn't take time for me to lose my mind,
saw that smile,
how I wish you were mine.
I try to look on the bright side,
not in my right mind,
every time I see a rose there's a vision of your face.
Here's what I know…
The day you became my friend,
I wished for and more,
I may wake to smile or maybe to cry,
the second I hear your voice,
I know an angel is near.
To my knees tears falling free,
God sent me an angel.
Here's what I know…
You're disagreeing or laughing.
If I had a problem plunging my mind,
it would take no time to suddenly disappear
and any pain, I seem to abandon.
Wish I could give you one more hug.
That's what I know.
You can disagree and laugh,
but it's not going to change what I know.

Each Other

As we take each other's hands,
we became the best of friends.
As our hearts joined together,
you took part inside my heart.
We find ourselves but far,
nothing could take us apart!
I stare towards the stars,
I see the great visions of your face.
I wish to give you that kiss upon your nose
in the silence of the night,
close your eyes,
everything standing still,
you can hear my voice.
Now you feel me squeezing you tight,
we see each other's smile.
Our hearts go wild!

Angels In My Dreams

Angels in my dreams,
watching over me tonight,
after bed time prayers,
nothing's brighter then their smile.
Hearts exploding, overflowing with tears,
but when all is silence,
they speak to me,
we are not just angels in your dreams.
We'll be by your side come morning light
and take you to the heavens after you die.
But until then we're with you day and night.

Fairytale 2

Isn't this beautiful, it's all the unthinkable!
It's so memorable, it's just not forgettable!
And every time I see your face
I feel that special place inside my heart,
close my eyes; I see that beautiful smile,
Angles holding us tight!
We hold each others' hearts inside.
We love to joke around and laugh.
Like a feather, we were floating in the wind.
Isn't this beautiful, it's all the unthinkable!
It's so memorable, it's just not forgettable!
It's just a measly little fairytale!

Forgiveness

Life comes and goes!
Reached my knees and falling free!
Though I must proceed,
I sit beneath the stars.
Let the tears fall as my heart stalls,
none begins to ease.
Eats through me upon my words,
I'm telling you no lies,
Further, I beg you to forgive me.
You disagree,
I fall to my knees,
I know I need you in my life.
Love at first sight,
I wish I was the only one holding you in life!

Goodbye

I'll never forget looking in your eyes,
could just see the two of us,
though it seems I'll never make you happy.
All I need is you to be right before my eyes,
you make it seem like heaven.
I would come running even if we found
ourselves many miles apart;
How I never want to say goodbye,
wish you would always be by my side.
Even though one day,
we may never see one another,
I can at least tell my kids,
I once knew this someone.
If you were to take a look you would think
she was sent from up above.
It's all a dream, even if everything was real,
I'll never be able to wipe that one last tear.
Always the fear it would be the last goodbye.
Never forget that you were always in my dreams.
You made my life worth living,
I hope the time never comes…..
I guess it's time for me too say goodbye.

Love

At night, I find myself to lay and cry,
and sometimes screaming out in pain,
but then it's too late.
Her love is more costly than diamonds,
more precious than gold;
This is no game, we found ourselves in love;
I can bring more misery than words can tell,
I can bring more happiness than you can explain,
it just depends on how you maintain.
If you dare have an affair,
go ahead; break up a correct love affair,
someone else is engaged in.
I'll bring more misery than words can tell!
The pain can be strong enough to kill,
only few are lucky to heal.
Respect life and never lie, be polite, attentive,
respectful and courteous;
I can bring more happiness than you can explain.
A lovely family, husband or wife,
ya'll tie the knot, enjoy life,
till ya'll grow old and die;
Either way, I'll give you a gift!

Toots 2

When you came into my life,
I lost my mind.
As time passed by,
you turned me right.
I love to see you before my eyes,
now it's all but a glare.
People were right; I should have cared more.
My actions were poor,
you deserve more;
I should not have made these mistakes.
This time it took me by the heart and tore me apart.
Now you have to fade away,
so I close my eyes to find you in my mind.
I try to sleep and there you are in my dreams,
all the memories won't ever set us free,
I hope this isn't the end.
I always believed true love could never be broken or ever stolen,
I'm on my knees, begging God, please…
You will never become a dream,
I still believe we're the perfect team,
until the day they lay us to rest.

Memory Lane

Take a trip down memory lane,
your mind goes blank,
everything used to be fine, big smiles and sunshine.
We were united as one and held each others' hands,
it was the best days of our lives.
We now define sorrow and pain right through our hearts.
We bleed each other's dreams; never will be the perfect team.
We can only imagine and dream,
if we were still united as one, big smiles and sunshine
is no longer in our minds;
We close our eyes, drop down, and cry,
let the tears drop down and dry.
Things will never be bright,
day or night, we still define sorrow and pain,
always express a frown and nothing more.

Morning Light

Morning light, but first come night,
I saw a gleam of stars in your eyes;
You were the one to reach into my heart.
All my life, I dreamed of meeting this special someone.
Going into this not knowing what I'll find,
decided to follow my heart,
and abandon my mind.
It was the rebirth of my heart,
your face became my morning light.
Just as soon as I thought,
all my dreams came crashing down;
You kept me from falling more,
and said it's not your imagination;
God loves you with all his heart,
and you're resting in his arms.
I am an angel
sent from the morning light;
You have just received me in your life.

By My Side

One thought that crosses my mind more than others
is how long both of us could possibly ever last?
Life is too fast, want to gasp for air,
and before your eyes, I know I never want to be alone,
it would only make me cry;
I'd only want to be with you that much more.
So sorry if I ever caused any pain,
what a disaster to see you gone.
I would only frown.
I would do anything to see you smile.
My love is always true.
Anything I'll do just to prove my love is true.
If we didn't make it last, just please forgive me this time.
Just take my life you're the only thing that runs through my mind
As time goes by....
I start to get tears right in my eyes
only because I failed to put a smile on your face,
so deep inside, I hope you won't say goodbye,
I need you by my side.
As time goes by, my love is always true.
Can't say it enough how much I love you,
words can't explain...
I'll always try my best to see you with a smile.
Anything to bring happiness!
I know it'll always be worth it to see you by my side.

Love For Ever

Our love is unconditional when we get emotional,
we only get stronger,
things couldn't be harder.
No way will we stay away, need you there with me by my side.
Will you always be mine, and stay inside my heart until we die?
I hope we start something new and never fight;
I'll give you all in sight and take you through the sky
with a big smile; your love drives me wild.
Close my eyes, I see you smile,
through the night you speak to me and stay deep within.
You're my number one above family and all,
I'll give it to you all,
I'll never fall only shine above all.
You are my one true love,
You make life complete,
and I'll always be there for you.

True love

Love is a blessing!
Can you see it's meant to be?
It's something that's deep and you're willing to keep,
it's that special someone you meet,
become the perfect team,
share each other's dreams,
and believe in one another.
You're beautiful and kind,
I'll look you in the eyes,
and tell you the truth,
not a single lie or ever break your heart.
I love you way to far;
I love to see you smile,
and I hate to ever see you cry.

In My Sight

To look in your eyes I could sit and cry,
no matter how much I try,
I know I want to be with you till the day I die.
I'll never lie, always want to keep you in my sight,
I have so much fright,
not of how much we fight,
but of you not staying in my sight.
Hardly ever fight,
and everything we ever do is just a joke.
So much love,
I hope you stay in my sight,
I want to take on life with you by my side.
Through thick and thin,
even then to have you by my side,
life will be worth the while,.
I hope you stay in my sight;
I'll make all the changes just to see you in my life.
I'll always see the two of us in my mind;
I'll keep you in my heart even if you decide to walk out of my life.
I hope our love never dies.

Babe

Babe, you're everything in my day!
I love to say how much you mean to me.
You're a blessing!
I hope we are high school sweethearts?
I hope you never become the past
and you always stay in my heart.
I hope one day,
I can give you the sky
and always tuck you in at night with a good night kiss.
I pray every night that you won't leave me?
Everything you give me makes it seem
as if I'm in a dream.
I hope you will always be inside of me
and you never fade away?
I just want you to love me, nothing more.
To be with you is the best thing than anything in the world.
You are my only true love!

I Found Love

If you're gone or find yourself kind of far,
in the light or in the night,
have no fright,
keep your heart bright,
and I'll always be in your sight.
Then you'll keep me in your thoughts
and you'll never be lost.
Although you tell me not to worry,
life's blurry with all the worries.
We can't tell a story that has no worries
but your kisses make me have no worries.
The way you treat me makes me think you're a queen.
You touch me deep down,
you never make me sad, frown, or cry.
You give me a crown, therefore you are my queen,
and all your kisses make me miss you twice as much.
Before your eyes, I've never lied;
I will always cry nor never deny my true love.
The day I get left, is the day I will have nothing to live for
but twice as better our hearts beat as one,
I really do love you.

Prayer

Trust the ones you love,
ignore the ones that dislike you,
take your hands and make a prayer;
Ask for those who don't believe,
so let's take a knee lightly;
Close your eyes and take the hands of the ones you love.
Dear father,
I've come today to ask about those who won't let us choose our fate,
they want to take our life by making us go different ways,
but you have not said it's time for us,
and when the time comes, please have her by my side.
I ask you to keep a close eye until we walk away or die.
I can say I go to church and in God I do trust,
even though we have both sinned, forgive the both of us.
I know you're willing to forgive;
We both have been blessed and saved in many ways.
You have always said forgive those who trespass against us,
as we can only pray for all of those
who choose to do so against us.
In Jesus name;
We pray,
Amen .

For Ever Last Our Love

I know your going to be the one always in my life.
I love you way to high!
Would love to sit and watch the sky and those beautiful bright stars.
You'll never put me to shame,
I hate it when we have a conflict,
it makes me feel like a failure.
I forgot to treat you right, have not a single doubt,
I'd hate to make us a dream,
I'd like to keep you in my life until the day I die.
I hope we get to tie the knot,
I'll love to be with you for the years to come.
I pray to God we stay strong.
I face the fear one day you won't be there,
I hope there's never a second thought.
I just want to take you somewhere you've never been.
It's a place that can't be seen, it's deep inside not in my mind,
just to find it can't be blind, you have to say you love one another.
Believe in each other to uncover all the love in each other.
Forever last our love till the day we die!

The Two of Us

When I hold your hand it's just like a fantasy for the two of us;
I know I never want to set you free or ever see you leave.
Just believe in the two of us!
I wish I could only fulfill your dreams!
I know it seems like one big dream,
you and I were never a dream;
It was always meant to be the two of us.
Before I ever go without you,
I need to make sure you and I understood each other;
I don't ever want to fall apart or ever say you were a dream.
All I mean is you were really perfect for me.
All I can think of is the two of us to the very end,
though all things must come to an end,
only the two of us can choose to go to the end.
I'll always believe in the two of us,
even when you wish to say bye or even just turn around and walk away.
I'll never forget when you and I were together,
you'll always be in my dreams,
even after one of us chooses to walk away.

Stop and Pray

I stop and pray, Lord
Watch over us.
Good or bad, guide us through your path.
Heaven or Hell,
keep us in your heart,
day or night, rain or shine, take care of us.
In Jesus name;
We pray;
Amen.

Better to Dream

I've seen you cry,
I've also seen you smile.
I know you think I'm lying
but I've seen it with my eyes.
Now you're thinking.....
"Why is he starring at me?"
So I simply reply,
"It's your lovely smile."
wish we could hold hands
and walk the sky together.
But instead,
I'll have dreams about being together
its better.
Can't disagree and argue,
date or separate,
nor ever get married
and taking the chance on ending the marriage.
Only ridding in our carriage without any worries
where I can always feel your lips
smiling when we kiss.

Heart

When it comes to love,
we tend to let our heart
believe that words are stronger
than our heart,
so it's easy to see
how people are torn apart.

My Shining Star

The poems you have just read are true and real,
the feelings were really there.
A young lady changed my life back in 2004,
so for you guys who say women make your life misery,
I have to disagree and ya'll just have to open your eyes and see.
This young lady has no idea how she set me free!
Even if my heart broke in two; one for the Earth to be stepped on,
and the other for her;
The days we spent together brought me together,
and I just want you to remember…
I hold you dearly deep inside my heart,
as I have from the start.
I'll love you forever,
with all my heart!
I'll always see your face,
sparkle with the stars.

Thank You!!

Index of Poems

Printed in the United States
77292LV00005B/571-720

9 781434 310835